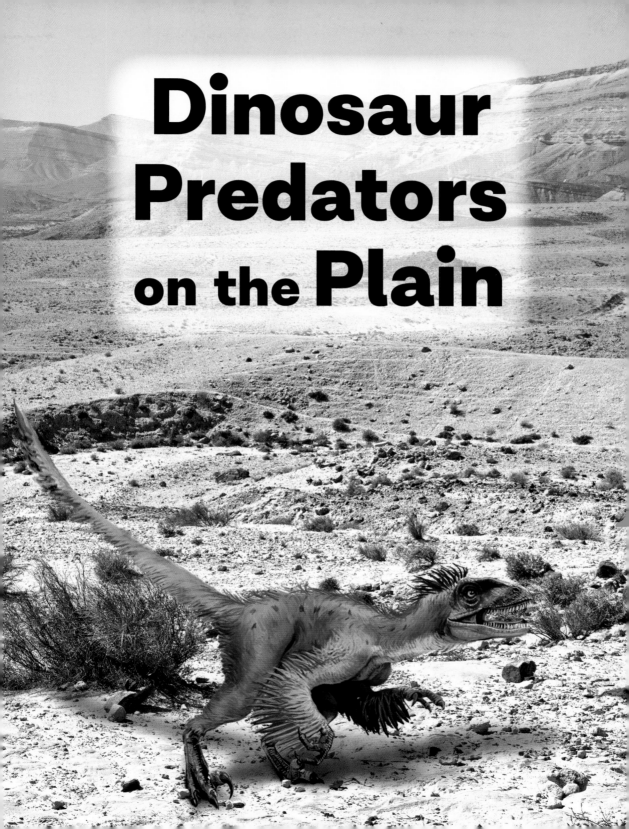

Dinosaur Predators on the **Plain**

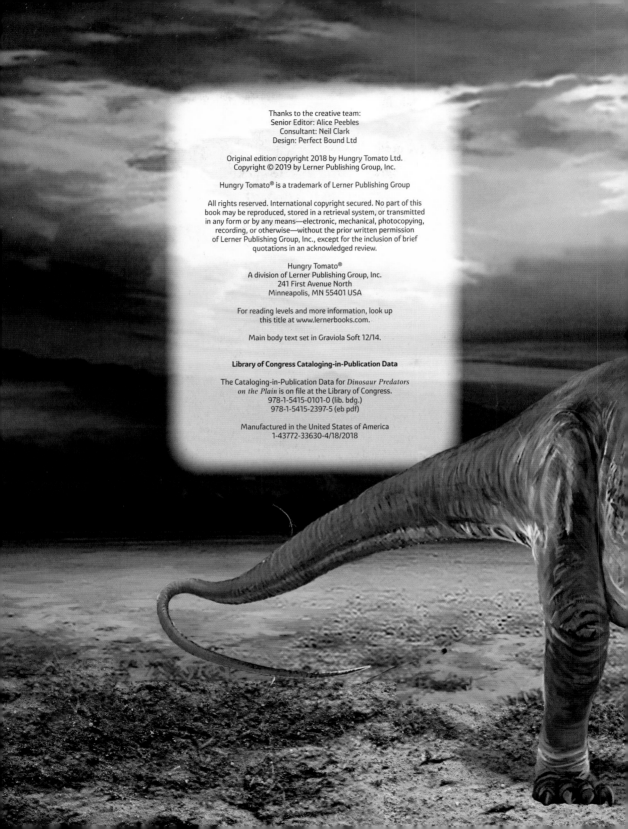

Thanks to the creative team:
Senior Editor: Alice Peebles
Consultant: Neil Clark
Design: Perfect Bound Ltd

Hungry Tomato®
A division of Lerner Publishing Group, Inc.
241 First Avenue North
Minneapolis, MN 55401 USA

For reading levels and more information, look up
this title at www.lernerbooks.com.

Main body text set in Graviola Soft 12/14.

Library of Congress Cataloging-in-Publication Data

The Cataloging-in-Publication Data for *Dinosaur Predators
on the Plain* is on file at the Library of Congress.
978-1-5415-0101-0 (lib. bdg.)
978-1-5415-2397-5 (eb pdf)

Manufactured in the United States of America
1-43772-33630-4/18/2018

Dinosaur Predators on the Plain

by Paul Mason

Illustrated by Andre Leonard

HUNGRY TOMATO™

MINNEAPOLIS

Contents

Dinosaur Rulers

Dinosaurs ruled Earth for tens of millions of years. They lived for about 900 times as long as humans have been around.

During the age of the dinosaurs, they spread across the world and lived in different habitats. On the wide plains roamed giant plant-eaters—and the predators that hunted them.

Triassic world
(250–201 million years ago)

During the Triassic Period, a giant supercontinent called Pangea was the main land. Away from the coasts, Pangea was mostly covered in hot, dry plains.

Jurassic world
(201–145 million years ago)

In the Jurassic Period, Pangea gradually broke up and new continents formed. Many plains areas became warmer and wetter, and more plants began to flourish.

Cretaceous world
(145–66 million years ago)

The continents we know today began to form in the Cretaceous Period, and the first grasses, as found on modern prairies, grew. Fossilized dung shows that giant titanosaurs began to eat this grass.

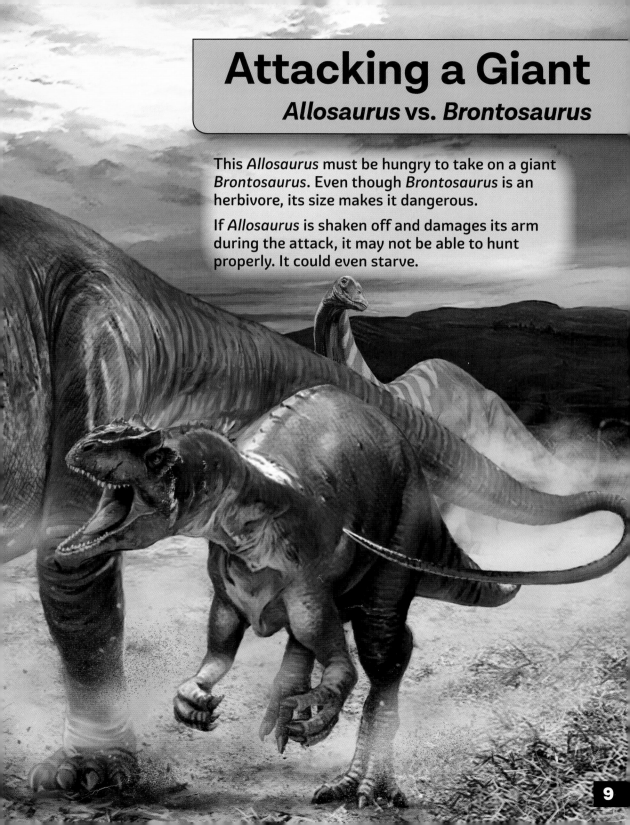

Attacking a Giant
Allosaurus vs. *Brontosaurus*

This *Allosaurus* must be hungry to take on a giant *Brontosaurus*. Even though *Brontosaurus* is an herbivore, its size makes it dangerous.

If *Allosaurus* is shaken off and damages its arm during the attack, it may not be able to hunt properly. It could even starve.

Allosaurus

Allosaurus was a tyrannosaur, a type of large predator that dominated during the Cretaceous Period. Groups of *Allosaurus* fossils have been found together, suggesting that this huge killer may have hunted in packs.

Compared to similar dinosaurs like *Tyrannosaurus*, *Allosaurus* had quite large arms. Some fossils have shown they were damaged, perhaps during attacks. *Allosaurus* may have used its arms when hunting, gripping hard as it bit into its prey.

SCALE

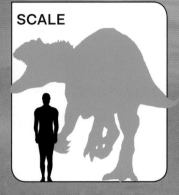

What's different?
Allosaurus means "different lizard." It was called this because its hourglass-shaped backbones were different from those of any other dinosaur then known.

FACT FILE

Alive: 155–150 million years ago
Order and Family: Saurischia/Allosauridae
Length: up to 39 ft. (12 m)
Height: 8 ft. (2.5 m)
Weight: 1.9 tons (1.7 t)
Diet: carnivorous
Fossils found: complete and partial skeletons and skulls
Location: Colorado, Utah, and Wyoming

Intrepid hunter
Fossil remains show *Allosaurus* sometimes hunted *Stegosaurus*, which was armed with dangerous tail spikes.

Brontosaurus

Slow digestion
It used to be thought that *Brontosaurus* swallowed stones to mash up food in their stomach. Experts now think this may not be the case.

The name *Brontosaurus* means "thunder lizard." This massive dinosaur grazed on dry floodplains and in river valleys. Its long neck allowed it to reach high-up vegetation and helped it spot predators.

Brontosaurus's main defense was its size: only the biggest predators would think they could kill it. It may also have used its long, flexible tail to swipe at attackers. Some experts think *Brontosaurus* could crack its tail like a whip, making a loud warning sound.

KILLER FACT

People used to think that *Brontosaurus* and another giant, *Apatosaurus*, were the same animal. Recently, though, experts decided they were different dinosaurs.

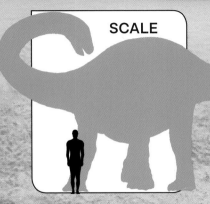

SCALE

FACT FILE

Alive: 155–150 million years ago
Order and Family: Saurischia/ Diplodocidae
Length: 72 ft. (22 m)
Height: 16 ft. (5 m)
Weight: 16.5 tons (15 t)
Diet: herbivorous
Fossils found: most of a skeleton
Location: Wyoming and Colorado

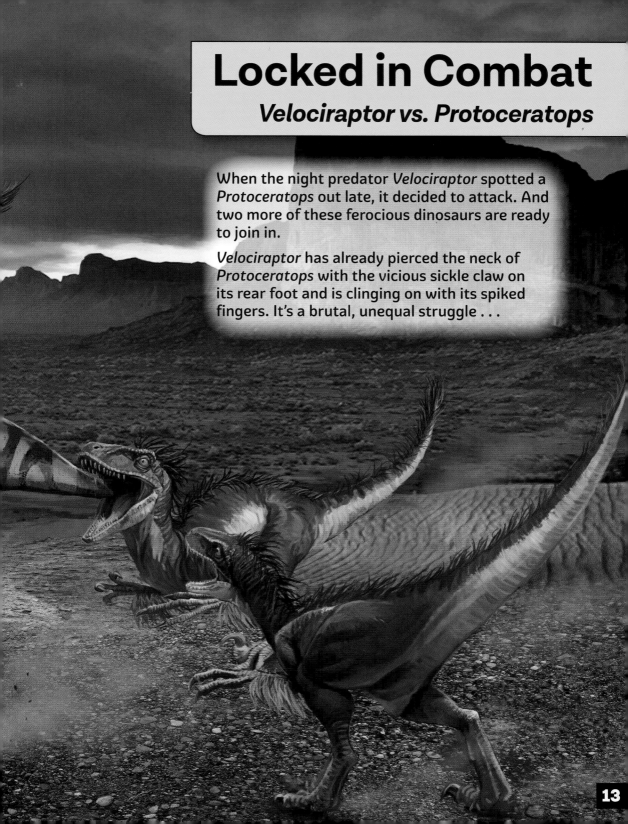

Locked in Combat
Velociraptor vs. Protoceratops

When the night predator *Velociraptor* spotted a *Protoceratops* out late, it decided to attack. And two more of these ferocious dinosaurs are ready to join in.

Velociraptor has already pierced the neck of *Protoceratops* with the vicious sickle claw on its rear foot and is clinging on with its spiked fingers. It's a brutal, unequal struggle . . .

Velociraptor

Velociraptor was a relatively small, fast-moving predator that probably hunted mainly at night. Its arms had feathers and would have looked like wings, though *Velociraptor* could not fly. Its legs were armed with a sickle claw: a large, hook-shaped claw on one toe that could stab at prey while its hands gripped on.

KILLER FACT

Like other swift hunting dinosaurs, *Velociraptor* had a long, stiff tail that stuck out behind. This helped it to balance during high-speed chases.

Fast attacker?

Velociraptor's name means "speedy thief." It could probably run at 24 mph (39 km/h), but was not one of the quickest dinosaurs. The ornithomimids could reach 37 mph (60 km/h).

Feathers?

Velociraptor is known to have had feathers on its "wings." Experts are not sure how much of the rest of its body was covered in them.

SCALE

FACT FILE

Alive: 75–71 million years ago
Order and Family: Saurischia/ Dromaeosauridae
Length: 8 ft. (2.5 m)
Height: 20 in. (50 cm)
Weight: 55 lb. (25 kg)
Diet: carnivorous
Fossils found: skeletons and skulls, so every part of this dinosaur is known
Location: Mongolia and northern China

Protoceratops

Protoceratops was a small herbivore that grazed mainly during the day. Fossils of this dinosaur are often found together, so it is likely that it lived in herds.

Protoceratops had a large head for its overall size. This may have been because it needed powerful jaw muscles for chomping down on tough plants—as well as chomping down on predators.

Grinding teeth
Protoceratops had lots of teeth in its upper and lower jaws. It used them to grind up plants it had bitten off with its powerful beak.

FACT FILE

Alive: 75–71 million years ago
Order and Family: Ornithischia/ Protoceratopsidae
Length: 8 ft. (2.5 m)
Height: 24 in. (60 cm)
Weight: 397 lb. (180 kg)
Diet: herbivorous
Fossils found: skeletons and skulls, so every part of this dinosaur is known
Location: Mongolia and northern China

Big families
In 2011, a *Protoceratops* nest with 15 young was found in Mongolia. This suggests that the dinosaur cared for its young after they hatched.

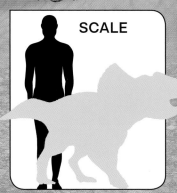
SCALE

15

These fully grown *Iguanacolossus* are a tough challenge for the *Utahraptors*. *Iguanacolossus* is much bigger, and a blow from its thumb spike could cause a nasty injury.

If the *Utahraptors* can separate out the young *Iguanacolossus*, though, they might be have a chance of bringing it down . . .

Utahraptor

Utahraptor was built large and strong, so it probably could not run as fast as more lightweight predatory dinosaurs. *Utahraptor* is likely to have hunted large prey by lying in wait, then bursting out and attacking.

Once it was within range, *Utahraptor* used its powerful leg muscles to stab its long sickle claw deep into its victim.

FACT FILE

Alive: 124 million years ago
Order and Family: Saurischia/Dromaeosauridae
Length: 20 ft. (6 m)
Height: 6 ft. (1.8 m)
Weight: 880 lb. (400 kg)
Diet: carnivorous
Fossils found: many different parts of the skeleton
Location: Utah

KILLER FACT

Did *Utahraptor* hunt in packs? In Utah, a group was found buried with an iguanodont. They may have chased it into quicksand and all died together.

SCALE

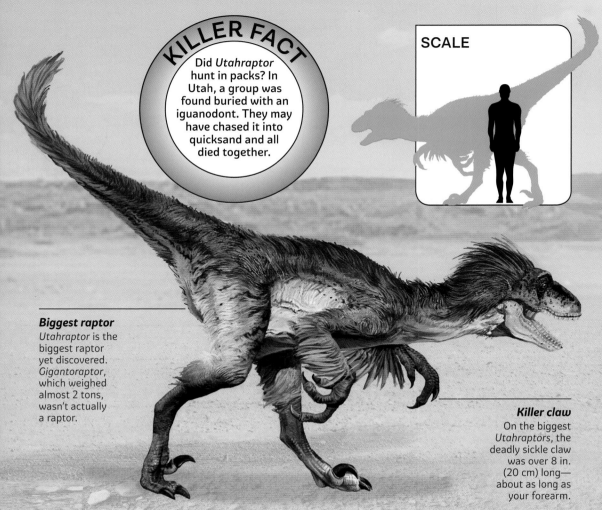

Biggest raptor
Utahraptor is the biggest raptor yet discovered. *Gigantoraptor*, which weighed almost 2 tons, wasn't actually a raptor.

Killer claw
On the biggest *Utahraptors*, the deadly sickle claw was over 8 in. (20 cm) long—about as long as your forearm.

Iguanacolossus

KILLER FACT

Iguanadonts like *Iguanacolossus* had a bony thumb spike sticking out of their wrist. The spike may have been used as a defensive weapon.

Iguanodont dinosaurs like *Iguanacolossus* were found grazing almost everywhere during the early Cretaceous Period. But *Iguanacolossus* was unusual because it was so large—between two and five times as heavy as most other iguanodonts. Huge dinosaurs like this were a challenge for many predators, which probably preferred smaller, easier meals.

Well balanced
Iguanacolossus had a spine and tail stiffened by bony structures. This helped it to balance on two legs.

SCALE

FACT FILE

Alive: 124 million years ago
Order: Ornithischia
Length: 30 ft. (9 m)
Height: 9 ft. 6 in. (2.9 m)
Weight: 5.5 tons (5 t)
Diet: herbivorous
Fossils found: parts of a skull and skeleton
Location: Utah

Long arms
Iguanodonts had very long arms, and probably walked on all fours as well as two legs.

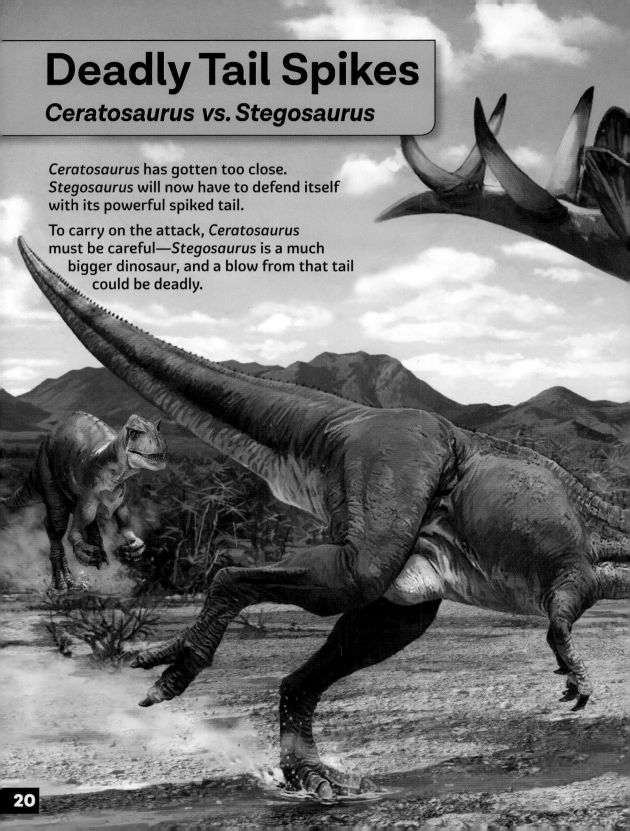

Deadly Tail Spikes
Ceratosaurus vs. Stegosaurus

Ceratosaurus has gotten too close. *Stegosaurus* will now have to defend itself with its powerful spiked tail.

To carry on the attack, *Ceratosaurus* must be careful—*Stegosaurus* is a much bigger dinosaur, and a blow from that tail could be deadly.

Ceratosaurus

Ceratosaurus is easy to spot because of the horn on its snout and its long teeth. Its teeth were like blades and were probably used for slashing at prey.

Ceratosaurus was an ambush predator, either lying in wait or sneaking up on possible victims. It had short, strong arms that may have been used for gripping prey.

SCALE

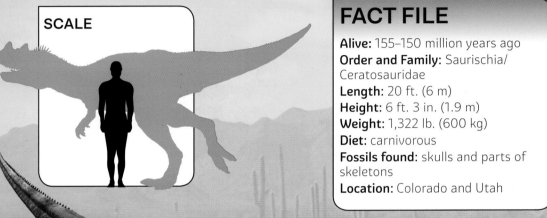

FACT FILE

Alive: 155–150 million years ago
Order and Family: Saurischia/ Ceratosauridae
Length: 20 ft. (6 m)
Height: 6 ft. 3 in. (1.9 m)
Weight: 1,322 lb. (600 kg)
Diet: carnivorous
Fossils found: skulls and parts of skeletons
Location: Colorado and Utah

Mystery horn
No one is sure what *Ceratosaurus*'s small horn was for. It was probably not strong enough to be a weapon, so it may have been used for display.

Water hunter?
Ceratosaurus had a flexible tail, similar to a modern crocodile's. Some experts think it may have hunted in rivers as well as on land.

Stegosaurus

Stegosaurus was certainly an unusual-looking dinosaur. Its back was lined with plates sticking up into the air. They were most likely arranged in two alternating rows (a plate on one side, followed by one on the other). The plates were lightweight and may have been able to change color, like a chameleon's skin.

KILLER FACT

Stegosaurus's main weapon was its spiked tail. The tail's swing may have been turbo-charged by a chemical called glycogen, stored near the base.

Thagomizer

Experts named the tail after a Gary Larson cartoon, in which a caveman professor explains, "This end is called a thagomizer, after the late Thag Simmons."

Not so big

Some experts think *Stegosaurus*'s back plates made it look bigger (and therefore harder to kill) to predatory dinosaurs.

FACT FILE

Alive: 155–152 million years ago
Order and Family: Ornithischia/ Stegosauridae
Length: 21 ft. (6.5 m)
Height: 11 ft. (3.5 m)
Weight: 3.9 tons (3.5 t)
Diet: herbivorous
Fossils found: two skulls and several skeletons, so every part of this dinosaur is known
Location: Colorado, United States; Portugal

Lost and Alone

Deinonychus vs. *Tenontosaurus*

This young *Tenontosaurus* has made a fatal mistake: it has been separated from the rest of its group.

Several *Deinonychus* are closing in for the kill, and *Tenontosaurus* doesn't know which way to turn. An attack by one *Deinonychus* would have little chance— but together, they may be successful.

Deinonychus

Deinonychus was a small, fast, ambush-and-pursuit predator that probably chased and ambushed its prey. Its narrow snout and forward-facing eyes were designed for seeing the exact distance to its prey.

Strong muscles in its jaw meant Deinonychus could bite through bone. Its tail could bend side to side but was held rigidly straight for balance while running.

Feathers
Other members of the same dinosaur family—older Microraptor and younger Velociraptor—had feathers, so experts think Deinonychus very likely did too.

Gator bite
Bite marks on Tenontosaurus fossils show that Deinonychus could probably bite with about the same force as a modern-day alligator.

SCALE

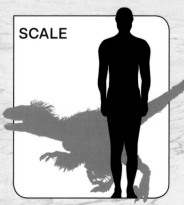

FACT FILE

Alive: 115–108 million years ago
Order and Family: Saurischia/Dromaeosauridae
Length: 10 ft. 9 in. (3.3 m)
Height: 3 ft. 3 in. (1 m)
Weight: 154 lb. (70 kg)
Diet: carnivorous
Fossils found: most of several skulls and skeletons

Tenontosaurus was one of the most common herbivorous dinosaurs in the early Cretaceous Period. It probably lived in a variety of places, from dry plains to river deltas, grazing on low- and mid-level plants wherever it could find them.

Tenontosaurus had an unusually long tail, which it could use for balance when standing up on two legs to reach food growing high up.

Long tailed
The tail made up over half the dinosaur's total length. It was held off the ground by strong muscles.

Four legs or two?
With long forelimbs and strong fingers, *Tenontosaurus* could have easily walked on all fours. It probably stood on two legs just to reach up for food.

FACT FILE

Alive: 120–100 million years ago
Order: Ornithischia
Length: 20 ft. (6 m)
Height: 5 ft. (1.5 m)
Weight: 1.1 tons (1 t)
Diet: herbivorous
Fossils found: many complete skulls and skeletons
Location: Montana, Texas, and Wyoming

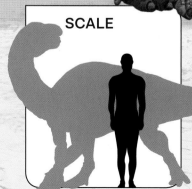
SCALE

Believe It or Not!

Pre-dinosaur Earth was hot, hot, hot!

Before the Triassic Period, temperatures were much higher than today. In fact, some scientists think that temperatures were so high that most life on Earth had been wiped out by the start of the Triassic—before dinosaurs began to take over. No wonder there were so many desert plains back then.

Giant dinosaurs ate (half) a ton!

Some scientists think the biggest dinosaurs— giant sauropods such as *Brontosaurus*—needed to eat up to half a ton of food *every day*.

Dinosaurs may have warmed the world

Having cooled down during the Jurassic Period, Earth's temperatures began to rise again. Some writers have suggested herbivorous dinosaurs may have contributed to this by releasing methane, a greenhouse gas, when they passed gas.

NATURAL GAS

Stegosaurus had a tiny brain

Even for a dinosaur, *Stegosaurus* was a bit dim. The smartest dinosaurs had brains about 70 percent as powerful as a bird's. *Stegosaurus* was much dumber: it had a brain about the size of ping-pong ball.

Triceratops had a *lot* of teeth

Not only did it have up to 40 teeth in both its upper and lower jaws, but behind each tooth were up to four more. They were replacements, ready for when the tooth wore out or broke. No wonder *Triceratops* teeth are common fossils.

Allosaurus might have eaten its prey alive

Some experts think *Allosaurus* ate by taking bites out of live prey, then leaving it to recover so that it could provide another meal in the future.

Paleontologists aren't perfect

Palaeontologists are dinosaur scientists. They research dinosaur fossils and use them to recreate dinosaurs. One of the first was Gideon Mantell (1790–1852). When he discovered the first iguanodont dinosaur, he thought its thumb spike was a nose horn.

Dinosaur Puzzlers

The dinosaurs may have died out, but there are still lots of curious, what-if questions to ask about them! Here are just a few . . .

Could dinosaurs survive on Earth today?

Some dinosaurs might be able to survive today—but it wouldn't be likely.

Earth is generally a lot cooler than when dinosaurs were around, which would make it hard—or even impossible—for most to survive. Humans now take up a lot of space, so there isn't really room for dinosaurs anymore. And they may not have had resistance to modern viruses and bacteria.

Is the Loch Ness Monster a dinosaur?

The Loch Ness Monster is said to live in a cold lake in Scotland. It's sometimes claimed to be a plesiosaur, a secret survivor from the dinosaur age.

The Loch Ness Monster is definitely *not* a dinosaur—plesiosaurs weren't dinosaurs. Even so, could a few plesiosaurs have survived, and carried on living secretly in deep lakes?

The answer's still no. Plesiosaurs probably needed warm, tropical waters to survive, but Loch Ness is very cold. And most importantly, there is no evidence that the Loch Ness Monster actually exists.

If dinosaurs had not died out, would we be here?

When a group of animals becomes extinct, its food sources and territory are available to others. The dinosaurs' disappearance created room for other animals to spread out.

One type of animal that became more widespread was mammals. They were already around, but were mostly active at night. After the dinosaurs disappeared they began to operate during the day. Mammals also became bigger and spread into new territories.

No one can know for sure, but if mammals had not developed in this way, humans probably would not have evolved. So if the dinosaurs hadn't died out, we might not be here.

Are there undiscovered dinosaurs living in remote parts of the world?

No, there aren't.

Even if dinosaurs could have adapted to the modern climate, humans have spread to every part of the planet and found no evidence of undiscovered dinosaurs.

Index

The Author

Paul Mason is a prolific author of children's books, many award-nominated, on such subjects as 101 ways to save the planet, vile things that go wrong with the human body, and the world's looniest inventors. Many contain surprising, unbelievable, or just plain revolting facts. Today, he lives at a secret location on the coast of Europe, where his writing shack usually smells of drying wetsuit (he's a former international swimmer and a keen surfer).

The Illustrator

Andre Leonard trained at Camberwell art school in London and at Leicester University. He has illustrated prolifically for leading magazines and book publishers, and his paintings are in a number of private collections worldwide. Andre prefers to work digitally but sometimes combines this with traditional media. He lives in Stamford, UK, with his wife, children, and a cat called Kimi, and he loves flying and sailing.

Glossary

ambush: surprise attack from an unseen position

carnivorous: living on a diet of meat. Carnivorous dinosaurs probably all hunted for food, though some may also have eaten already-dead animals.

family: label given to groups of dinosaurs that had similar physical characteristics but were not exactly alike

fossil: remains of a living thing from long ago. Fossils can be the remains of bones, shells, pieces of wood, and plants—there are even fossilized footprints.

herbivorous: living on a diet of plants. Herbivorous dinosaurs would have been most plentiful wherever there was a good supply of plants and water.

order: one of two groups of dinosaurs, which were divided based on the way their hips worked

Ornithischia: one of the two orders of dinosaur. Ornithischian dinosaurs were "bird-hipped," with hips that looked similar to a bird's.

Saurischia: one of the two orders of dinosaur. Saurischian dinosaurs were "lizard-hipped," with hips that looked like a modern lizard's.

sauropod: one of the kinds of Saurischians, lizard-hipped dinosaurs. Sauropods had long necks and tails, small heads, and large bodies with four thick legs.

sickle: curved shape, with a pointed end. Some sickles also have a knife-like edge on their inside curve.

Picture credits

t= top, b= bottom, l = left, m = middle, r = right.

Shutterstock: Abakz 29tr; Henk Bentlage 31tr; Gustavo Frazao 28br; Harvepino 30tl; David Herraez Calzada 29tl; plena 7r; Zeljko Radojko 28tr.

5